The American Spirit

By Dean Walley

Illustrated by
Noreen Bonker, Steve Carter,
Skip Damon, David R. Miles,
and Ginny Scott

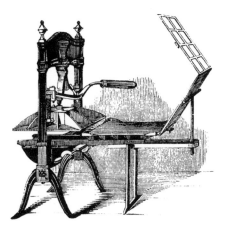

Hallmark Crown Editions

Photographic Credits: Pages 24-25, 30-31, Culver Studios. Page 36(C) Courtesy Library of Congress. Pages 36(T), 40, reproduced by courtesy of the National Aeronautics and Space Administration. *Acknowledgment:* Excerpt from "I Have a Dream" by Martin Luther King, Jr. Reprinted by permission of Joan Daves. Copyright © 1963 by Martin Luther King, Jr.

I am an American.

I have come from the four corners
                    of the earth...
        ...in flight from the old
and the ruined and the oppressive.
I have come to the Golden Door...
        ...in search of Freedom.

I have been poor...
        ...and tired
                ...and homeless
...but I have found a wealth
        of the spirit, a strength of will,
a home at last...

...in this new world of tall mountains
and virgin timber and broad prairies.

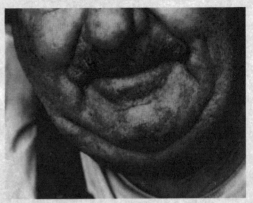

I am an American.
I am many different things...
            but in these differences
there is a sameness of belief.
    For I believe in myself...
            ...in the destiny of this land.

I believe...

...that all men are created equal,

that they are endowed by their Creator

with certain inalienable rights,

that among these are life, liberty

and the pursuit of happiness.

I am an American.
I have crossed the prairies
        and the mountains
            in a covered wagon...
        ...living mostly on hope
            ...charting the unknown
                ...sleeping under the stars.

I have followed the sun
           in search of gold...
and found a greater prize
           in new lands...
  ...in the brave hearts
       of my fellows.

I have lived in a house
        divided by war...
and in honoring my fallen brothers
I have spoken from my heart...

QUOTATIONS

Page 10: From the *Bill of Rights*.
Page 17: Abraham Lincoln, *Gettysburg Address*.
Page 34: Martin Luther King, Jr., speech
at Washington, D.C.—August 28, 1963.
Page 37: Edward M. Kennedy
quoting George Bernard Shaw
in the eulogy of Robert F. Kennedy.
Page 39: John F. Kennedy, *Inaugural Address*.
Page 41: Neil Armstrong, first words from the
moon—July 20, 1969.
Page 45: Walt Whitman, *Leaves of Grass*.

The artists made many of their
own color separations for this book
and closely supervised the printing
for utmost accuracy of reproduction.
The type is set in Caslon Old Style,
a typeface originally designed by William Caslon
after Dutch types of the late seventeenth century.
The paper is Hallclear, White Imitation Parchment,
and Ivory Fiesta Parchment.
The cover is bound with natural weave book cloth
and Torino paper. Book design by David R. Miles.
The designer gratefully acknowledges the assistance
of Gary Peltier in preparing this edition.

Page 10: From the Bill of Rights.
Page 17: Abraham Lincoln, Gettysburg Address.
Page 34: Martin Luther King, Jr. speech
at Washington, D.C.—Aug. 28, 1963.
Page 37: Edward M. Kennedy,
quoting George Bernard Shaw
in the eulogy of Robert F. Kennedy.
Page 30: John F. Kennedy, Inaugural Address.
Page 41: Neil Armstrong, first words from the
moon—July 20, 1969.
Page 45: Walt Whitman, Leaves of Grass

The artists made many of their
own color separations for this book
and closely supervised the printing
for utmost accuracy of reproduction.
The type is set in Caslon Old Style,
a typeface originally designed by William Caslon
after Dutch types of the late seventeenth century.
The paper is Halliclear, White Imitation Parchment,
and Ivory Foam Parchment.
The cover is bound with natural weave look cloth
and Torino paper. Book design by David K. Miles.
The designer gratefully acknowledges the assistance
of Gary Felder in preparing this edition.

I am an American!

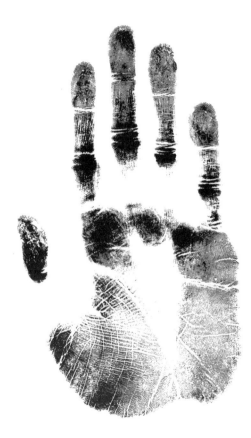

I am the farmer at his plow.
I am the mother with her child.
I am the merchant in his shop.
I am the statesman, the soldier, the minister,
the child, the poet, the philosopher,
the builder, the lover....
I am two hundred million people.
I am one spirit.

...*magnificent masses*

careless of particulars

...*the roughs, beards, friendliness,*

combativeness...

...*the soul loves.*

...*the flowing trains, the crowds, equality,*

diversity...

...*the soul loves.*

I move freely through its vastness
and all about me I see...

I am an American.
This land of mine is the greatest poem.
It is a poem of life and work,
    love and sacrifice, sorrow and joy.

I am an American.
I feel great pride
and at the same time
    I am humble enough
to walk for the first time on the moon
and count that achievement as...

...one small step for a man,

one giant leap for mankind.

I am an American...
and I say...

...*Ask not what your country*

can do for you...

ask what you can do for your country!

I am an American...
and I want to work and live and dare
to make my country
        all that it can be, for...

   ...*some men see things as they are*

   and say, why?

I dream things that never were

   and say, why not?

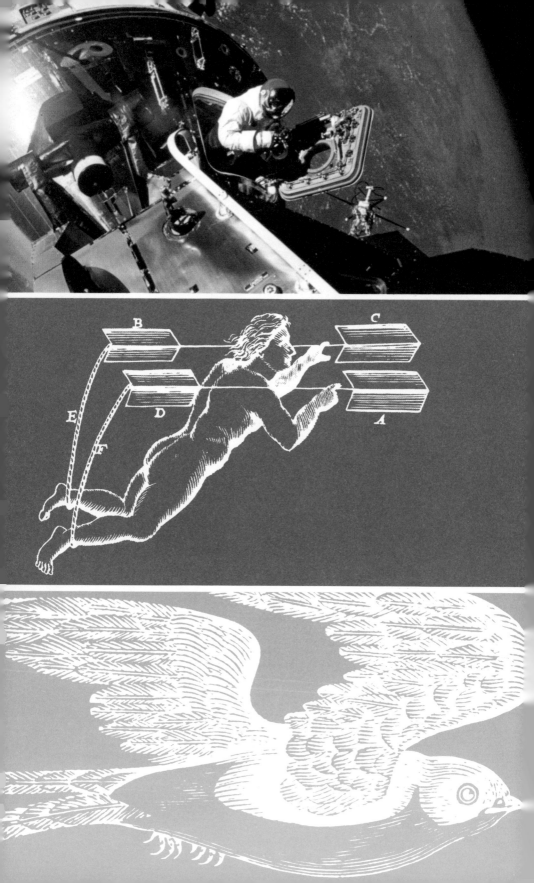

I am an American...
and I have a dream...
a dream of a time when we...

...will be able to join hands and sing...,

"Free at last! free at last!

thank God almighty,

we are free at last!"

There are moments in my past I view
with great pride...
...and there are scenes
that cry out in my memory.
But only in realizing the good
and the bad that has gone before
can I become the American
I must be in the days ahead.

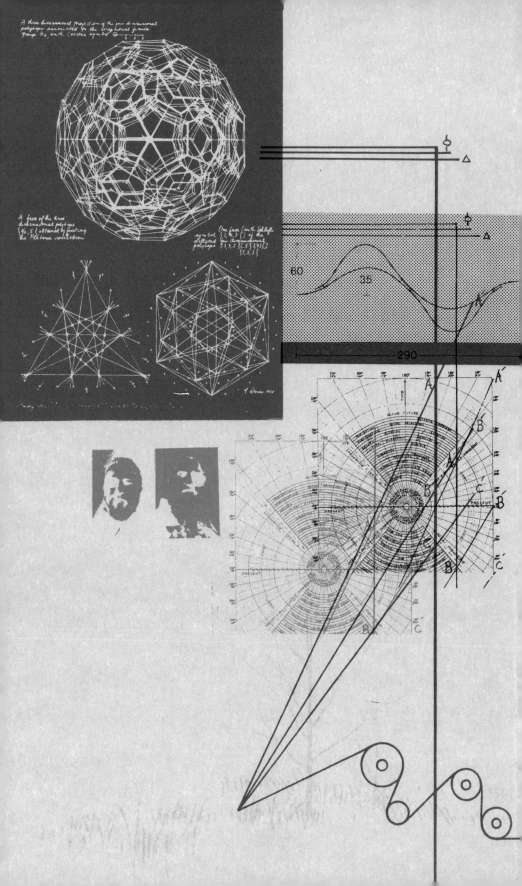

I have planted trees...
   ...and I have laid waste
   to the land I love.

...I have lived in the darkness
of the ghetto where the sun never shines.

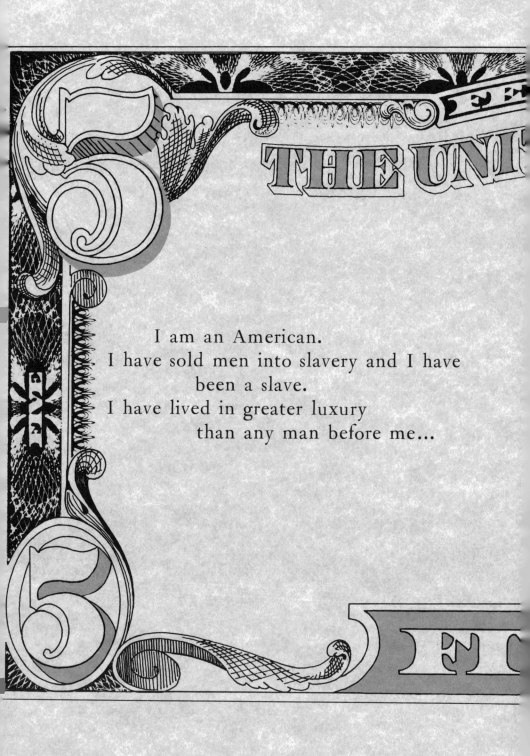

I am an American.
I have sold men into slavery and I have
been a slave.
I have lived in greater luxury
than any man before me...

But there is in me a thing
          that knows no death,
and my spirit is living still
in the land of the free
          and the home of the brave.

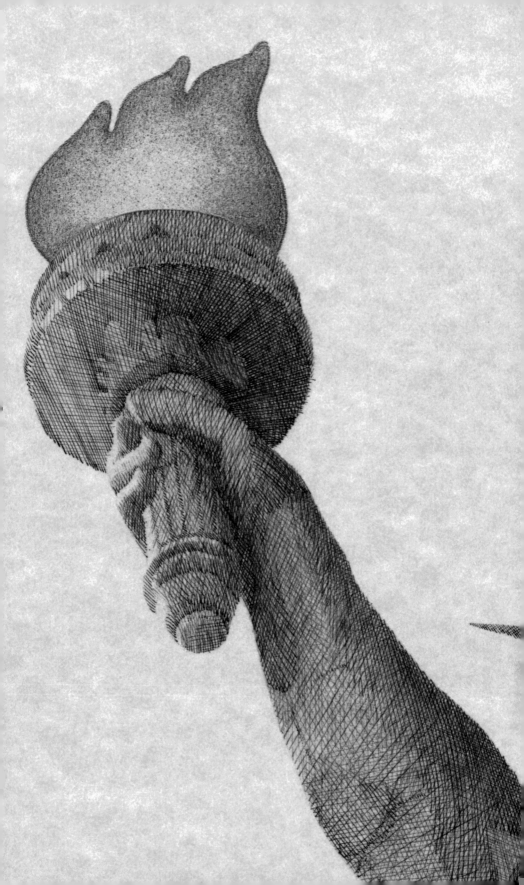

I have given my life so many times
for my country...
...at Valley Forge...Appomattox
...Belleau Wood
...Iwo Jima...Da Nang.

I am as old as Man's love of Freedom...
I am as young as tomorrow.

I worship in churches, cathedrals,
    synagogues, temples,
        rude tents and wild forests.

...from the heart of America,
with high resolve...

...that these dead

shall not have died in vain;

that this nation, under God, shall have

a new birth of freedom;

and that government

of the people,

by the people,

for the people,

shall not perish from the earth.

I am an American.
I speak in diverse accents.
My skin has many hues.

BI